# Arise and Shine,
# For Thy Light Has Come

# Arise and Shine, For Thy Light Has Come

Regina C. Njoku

authorHOUSE®

*AuthorHouse™*
*1663 Liberty Drive*
*Bloomington, IN 47403*
*www.authorhouse.com*
*Phone:1-800-839-8640*

*First published by AuthorHouse    09/20/2011*

*ISBN:978-1-4670-0130-4 (sc)*
*ISBN:978-1-4670-0131-1 (ebk)*

*Printed in the United States of America*

*Any people depicted in stock imagery provided by Thinkstock are models, and such images are being used for illustrative purposes only.*
*Certain stock imagery © Thinkstock.*

*This book is printed on acid-free paper.*

# Contents

# Dedication

I dedicate this book to the Holy Spirit my teacher, my comforter and the source of my joy.

I thank you father for giving me the gift of the spirit of "Nothing is impossible".

I thank you father for loving me and giving me the opportunity to have a test of your love.

I thank you father for making me wonderfully and fearfully, in your likeness and image.

I thank you father for giving me access into your presence which makes me live the book of Isaiah 40:31;—

"But they that wait upon the LORD shall renew their strength; they shall mount up with wings as Eagles;

They shall run and not be weary; and they shall walk, and not faint.

Father, I join all your creatures and say; you are worthy to be praised.

I join the host of heaven and say; all glory and honor be yours forever and ever, amen.

# Chapter 1

# We are made in His image and likeness.

God made us in His own image and likeness for us to be like Him:blameless, powerful and full of knowledge. He wants us to live a life full of happiness, a life without worries and a life spent in his presence, In reverence to his greatness.

He gave us dominion and unlimited power over the works of his hands. Let us take a look at the book of Genesis 1:26-27.

> God said, let us make man in our image, in the likeness
> Of ourselves and let them be masters of the fish of the
> Sea, the birds of heaven, the cattle, all the wild animals
> And the creatures that creep along the ground.
> God created man in the image of himself, in the image of
> God he created him, male and female he created them.

In the very beginning when God created man, his original intension is to take care of man so that man will dwell in the presence of God. He provided everything that man would ever have need for before creating man. He never wanted man to depend on himself for a living but to depend on what God has already provided for him.

God wants to have a relationship like the one between an earthly father and his child. He wants us to experience and live his love for us.

God has always given man a chance to be himself; a chance to make a choice, a chance to demonstrate his wisdom and knowledge, a chance to work in agreement. Just as recorded in the book of Genesis 2:12:—

> And out of the ground the Lord God formed every beast
> Of the field, and every fowl of the air, and brought them
> Unto Adam to see what he would call them:and whatsoever
> Adam called every living creature that was the name thereof.

God created every beast and every fowl of the air and took them To Adam because He wanted Adam to be part of what He was doing. God wanted Adam to demonstrate the authority which he has given him.

God's intension for man has never changed, because he is God and he will never change. But unfortunately, things are no longer the way God intended them to be. Man has wondered so far away from God and has lost his ways. Man now depends completely on what he can do for himself. Permit me to use this human example for what is happening between God and His children.

I want you to think of your childhood, how your parents cared for you and wouldn't let anything harm you, how hard they worked to put food on your table despite all odds. They did all that because they had hoped that someday you'll grow up to be better than them or at least be like them. That was why they made you cry when it was necessary, they taught you not to lie but to be honest, paid your way through school, they did everything required of them as parents and now you're an adult. Thank God you've grown, but you've forgotten your parents. You don't ask about them. You don't honor them as your parents.

They've lost all hope concerning your love for them and their dreams and expectations are dead, all because they no longer hear from you. Anytime you remember them or someone else talks to you about them you'll say "Well, I know they're fine, I know it does not matter if they hear from me or not".

This illustration I've just given is not half way what we make the Lord God Almighty go through. It's not half way the manner we treat Him. We don't make Him the proud father he deserves to be. In most cases, we don't see him as the great provider of all things. We don't really realize that he can do exceedingly, abundantly, and above all we can think or ask of him. We are just like the woman at the well in the book of John 4:10. If only we know the gift of God and the things he has made available for us, we would just run back to him now.

It is time we rise from our slumber to accomplish the very first commandment God gave us in the book of Genesis chapter 1:28:—

> God blessed them, saying to them, "Be fruitful, multiply,
> Fill the earth and subdue it.

In case you did not understand this verse clearly, God has given you the power to be productive in every area of your life, to increase and to overcome whatsoever has come against you.

Like God said to Jeremiah in the book of Jeremiah 1:4-5:—

> Before I formed you in the womb I knew you;
> Before you came to birth I consecrated you;
> I appointed you as prophet to the nations.

That is how the day God formed you in your mother's womb and before you came to birth he has given you the power on the inside of you to be fruitful, multiply and to subdue. So it is time for you to stop acting like an orphan because your father is the king of Kings and the Lord of Lords. Jesus is your elder brother according to the book of Hebrews 2:16-17:—

> For verily he took not on him the nature of angels;
> But he took on him the seed of Abraham.
> Wherefore in all things it behooved him to be made
> Like unto his brethren, that he might be a merciful and
> High priest in things pertaining God, to make reconci-
>    liation for the sins of his people.

You also have the Holy Spirit as your teacher and the Angels of God as your servants according to the book of Hebrews 1:14:—

> Are they not all ministering spirits, sent to serve for the
>    sake of those who are to inherit salvation.

Get up!!!, sleeping time is over!!!. It's morning!!!. It's time for a new beginning, time to seek the Lord our God with everything about you, in spirit and in truth.

Get entangled with the word of God, study it like you've never done before, feed your spirit and soul with it.

The devil deceived Adam and Eve because they did not have perfect understanding of the word that God spoke to Adam. I can assure you that if you have the knowledge of the word of God, the devil cannot mess you up!.

The devil knows that when you have the knowledge of the word of God, the Holy Spirit, the spirit of truth begins to teach you to walk according to the ways of the Lord and then you find life. The book of Leviticus 18:5 says:—

> I Yahweh, am your God:hence you will keep my laws and
> my customs. Whoever complies with them will find
> life in them.

How can you keep the laws and customs of God if the Holy Spirit did not teach you? And how can the Holy Spirit teach you if you don't have the word of God deposited in you? But if you feed your mind with the word of God, since God says you'll find life in His word, this means you'll find Jesus because he is the way the truth and life.

God the father really wants us to inherit all the promises he made to our ancestors Abraham, Isaac and Jacob. That is why he sent his only begotten son according to the book of John 3:16.

> For God so loved the world:he gave his only begotten
> son,
> That whosoever believes in him may not perish but may
> have Eternal life.

This also takes us to the book of revelation 5:9-10:—
They sang a new hymn:

> You are worthy to take the scroll and break it's seals,
> Because you were sacrificed, and with your blood you
> Bought people for God of every race, language, people
>     and nation
> And made them a line of kings and priests for God to rule
>     the world.

When we accept Jesus as our Lord and savior and live our lives obeying the word of God, we are fulfilling God's heart desire. When we repent of our sins and come back to God our Father through Jesus our brother, we automatically join a line of kings and priests for God, and we actually make him happy because he knows we will not perish, his efforts to save us are not in vain. But our problem is that we try to seek God in our own ways. We always seek him only in times of need, when he is already far from us. That's why we have problems, stress, worries, and all the rest of it as stumbling blocks standing in—between us and him, and these things make it impossible for us to reach him. But if we act according to his instructions as he wants us to in the book of Matthew 6:33-34:—

> But seek ye first the kingdom of God, and his righteousness;
>     and all these things shall be added unto you.
> Take therefore no thought for the morrow: for the morrow
>     shall
> Take thought for itself. Sufficient unto the day is the day's
>     trouble.

This is what Jesus Christ the maker of life asks us to do; To seek first the kingdom of God and his righteousness. That means, presenting ourselves as living sacrifices unto our Holy God.

Let your heart desire be like that of King David in the book of Psalm 27:4

One thing have I desired of the Lord, that will I seek after; that I may dwell in the house of the Lord all the days of my life to behold the beauty of the Lord, and to inquire in his temple.

I can assure you that if you invest all the energy you use in searching for worldly solutions, in seeking the Lord's presence, you'll find him, then peace and every other thing shall he add unto you.

For this I invite you to say this prayer:—

> Lord Jesus come into my life, forgive me all my sins and
> short comings,
> I have sinned against you and have walked away from
> your ways,
> Wash me with your Precious blood of Jesus which was
> shed on the
> Cross of Calvary for my sake and restore me to yourself.
> Create in me a clean heart and renew the right spirit
> within me.
> I offer as a sacrifice to you my God, my broken and
> contrite heart.
> Restore unto me the joy that comes from your name, in
> Jesus name, Amen.

If you said this prayer with a sincere heart, know that the power in the blood of Jesus has been activated on your behalf. I also want you to know that the book of Romans 8:1 is standing by you. Let's read:—

> There is therefore now no condemnation
> To them which are in Christ Jesus,
> Who walk not after the flesh, but after the spirit.

Truly as God said, we perish for lack of knowledge. Since we don't really know the word of God, we cannot put them into action. So, cultivate the habit of reading the word of God because the more you read the word of God the more light you have in you and the more light you have in you is the more of Jesus Christ you have in you; because Jesus Christ is the light of the world, and every form of darkness in you He will put away. It's automatic.

Why was our Lord Jesus able to defeat the devil the three times he tempted him when he came out of the wilderness, after forty days of fast? Do you think he defeated the devil because he is Jesus Christ the son of the living God? Or maybe you think he defeated the devil because he came for that purpose.

Well, in case you don't know why. The only reason our Lord Jesus Christ defeated the devil is because He had the full knowledge of the word of God. He had the full knowledge of the word of God, not because he is Jesus Christ but because he took time to study the scripture!

Whatsoever you invest your time in, is what bears fruit for you. Every fruit reproduces it's kind! If you spend your time under hard work all through the day, at the end of the day you'll receive your pay. If you spend your time doing worthless things or the things that does not glorify the Lord, at pay time you'll receive disaster. So also if you invest your time in reading the word of God, you'll grow from knowledge to knowledge, you'll know when to talk and when not to, when to be still and when to act. It all depends on you because the power is within you.

The devil knows that once you start reading the word of God, it's over for him in your life! That is why he brings distractions so you will never find time to read the word of God, and if at all you find time to read it, you may never understand it because your mind is filled with thoughts of the flesh. So always remember that he comes as a roaring lion, but the one in you is the Lion of the tribe of Judah. He comes threatening to kill and destroy you, but don't worry, for the life you have in you is the breath of God, So the devil cannot get God out of you. God has the final say over every area of your life. He comes with failure and discouragement over your staff of bread, but rejoice because your hands are blessed and whatsoever you lay your hands on, shall prosper. He comes visualizing in your mind the reasons why you can never come out of debt and poverty, but be calm, you have nothing to fear because Christ Jesus became poor that you might be rich. Every single thing you might need as long as you live has been paid for in full.

But, how can you prove this things if you don't even know that they exist and are available for you

# Chapter 2

# Knowing God for Who He Really Is

God's heart desire is for us to know and love him as he has loved and shown his love for us, and also because he is our father. Not because he can do one thing or the other for us

When you come to know God the father through our Lord Jesus Christ, as you accept him as your Lord and savior, there must come a time when you might not fit in among your friends, there must come a time when you'll have to give up old things and make room for new ones, join the company of believers like you in other to share the word of God and learn more about God our father, Jesus our savior and the Holy spirit our helper.

At this point you'll have to do what Abraham did in the book of Genesis 21:8-14:—

> The child grew up and was weaned, and Abraham gave a great banquet on the day Isaac was weaned. Now Sarah watched the son that Hagar the Egyptian had borne to Abraham playing with her son Isaac. Drive away that slave—girl and her son she said to Abraham, this slave—girl's son is not to share the inheritance with my son Isaac. This greatly distressed Abraham, because the

slave—girl's child too was his son, but God said to him, do not distress yourself on account of the boy and your slave—girl. Do whatever Sarah says, for Isaac is the one through whom your name will be carried on. But the slave—girl's son I shall also make into a great nation, for he too is your child. Early the next morning, Abraham took some bread and a skin of water and giving then to Hagar, put the child on her shoulder and sent her away.

It is important for you to stay away from things that are not helping you grow in faith. If you want to grow in understanding, knowledge and wisdom in the things of the Lord God Almighty, you must have time to be alone with God through his word.

For Abraham, it was not an easy decision to take. But because God had spoken, he obeyed. That is how God wants us to walk with him:in obedience, trusting him because he is all knowing God. We should walk with Him knowing that his thoughts for us is for good and not for evil, to give us an expected end.

You have to demonstrate with physical and material things that you love and trust the Living God that you know God can take absolute care of you and that whatever you have was given to you by God and He can still provide more for you at any given time.

Sometimes we do not hear from the Lord because we are hanging out with some people whom we should not be hanging out with, because our characters or our ways of doing things are no longer the same. We must make separations like Abraham did and only after then will God the Father Almighty reveal the secret hidden things which we know nothing of, to us.

Let's take for instance Genesis 13:8, 14-18:-

> And Abraham said unto Lot, let there be no strife, I
> pray thee, between me and thee, and between my
> herdsmen and thy herdsmen; for we be brethren.
> And the Lord said unto Abram, after that Lot was
> separated from him, lift up thine eyes,
> And look from the place where thou art northward, and
> southward, and eastward, and westward:
> For all the land which thou seest, to thee will I give it, and
> to thy seed forever.
> And I will make thy seed as the dust of the earth:so that
> if a man can number the dust of the Earth, then shall
> thy seed also be numbered.
> Arise, walk through the land in the length of it and in the
> breadth of it; for I will give it unto thee. Then Abram
> removed his tent, and came to Mamre, which is
> Hebron, and built there an altar unto the Lord.

We must trust the Lord completely, without reservation before he can reveal himself to us. We must tell him we know he's in total control of everything taking place in our lives even if what is happening around us is different from what should be happening. We have to hold on, wait on the Lord.

What are you struggling with today? Which area of your life do you need to give up, knowing it does not glorify the Lord. Whatever it is, if you sincerely want to give it up, I ask you to present it as a sacrifice unto God the father and he will deliver you from it.

God knows and understands our weaknesses, pains and sorrows. That is why he said in the book of Isaiah 1:18:-

Come, let us talk this over, says the Lord.

Though your sins are like scarlet,

They shall be white as snow:

Though they are red as crimson, they shall be like wool.

If you are willing to obey, you shall eat the good things of
the earth.

But if you refuse and rebel, the sword shall eat you
instead—for

Yahweh's mouth has spoken.

You've heard from God's mouth. He does not care for whatever might have happened in the past, but he is asking you to give them up. He's waiting for you with open arms to wash your sins away and position you to eat the good things of the earth.

In most cases, many people think they've wondered so far away from God that they can no longer be restored. They feel they've committed too many sins and God has condemned them, and that the best thing they can do is to continue in sin, but you know what? That is the biggest lie of the devil! The devil has so corrupted the minds of the children of God that they think God gave us the Ten Commandments, or God wants us to keep ten laws when we can only keep two or three of it. No! The only one commandment God gave us is to love the Lord our God with all our heart, all our soul, all our strength and all our mind, with everything about us just as recorded in the book of Luke 10:27. When we obey this commandment, life is easy; our Christian walk becomes easy, light and enjoyable. God wants us to come to Him just like we are, then He will teach us through His word to live according to His standards. If God does not want us as sinners, why then did he send his only begotten son

Christ Jesus to die for our sins on the cross? The point is this; God wants us to come to him as sinners but He does not want us to continue with him in sin, he does not want us to fellowship with him as sinners but as sons and daughters of his. He does not want us to remain as we came to Him, that is why we must trust in his word, and then he will take us from glory to glory. You must Know that God loves you just the way you are, and as a proof for His love for us he sent his beloved son Jesus Christ our Lord and savior to die for us while we are still sinners. God wants us to come to him with our sins then he will cleanse us.

Let's take a look at the book of Hebrew 4:15-16:—

> For the high priest we have is not incapable of feeling our
> Weaknesses with us, but has been put to the test in exactly
> The same way as ourselves, apart from sin. Let us then, have no fear in
> Approaching the throne of grace to receive mercy and to find
> Grace when we are in need of help.

Jesus Christ is our high priest who feels our weaknesses with us and he is asking us to have no fear in coming to the throne of grace when we need help, since there is no other time we need grace more than when we are doing the will of God.

What God desires so much is our fellowship with him, but we cannot really fellowship with him if we do not take every obstacle out of the way.

If we are really determined to leave our old sinful lives, we must give in to God through his word and be ready to put every single word of God we hear into action, then resist the devil and he will flee away from us. You must also bear in mind that the nearer you draw to God, the nearer God draws to you. God our father is not a respecter of anyone; for what he did for one man he will do for another.

## Personal Encounter with Jesus

The secret behind having a personal encounter with Christ Jesus is by giving him first place in everything you do. Your thoughts, your decisions, your actions etc. He must come first. You must always be mindful of him. You must come to a point where nothing else matters to you like keeping his commandments. You must come to a point like apostle Paul in the book of Philippians 3:7-9:—

> But what were once my assets I now through Christ Jesus
>     count as losses.
> Yes, I will go further because of the supreme advantage
>     of knowing Christ
> Jesus my Lord, I count everything else as loss. For him I
>     have accepted the
> Loss of all other things, and look on them all as filth if
>     only I can gain Christ
> And be given a place in Him, with the uprightness I have
>     gained not from the
> Law, but through faith in Christ, as uprightness from God,
>     based on faith.

Whatever is in between you and God must go away. Idolatry does not necessarily mean you have another god you bow down to, or that you have charms which you believe in, but anything that hinders the move of God in your life is an idol.

I would also like to remind us that God is very much concerned with what we do in secret, what we do when no one is watching you because that is where you'll meet God "in the secret place". We are expected to work out our salvation with fear and trembling, knowing that God who sees in secret watches over us to pay us back according to our works.

The devil our greatest enemy has sown the seed of deception in the church, causing Christians to believe they cannot attain the level of holiness that God the father expects from us. We should always bear in mind that without holiness no man can see God.

We must approach God's throne of grace being conscious of his love for us, knowing we can do all things through Christ who strengthens us. We should also approach him knowing that it's not by might nor by power, but by the spirit of the Lord Zachariah 4; 6-7.

When we desire to live our lives out of sin and walk in holiness, we come to know that God is able to make all grace abound towards us, that we always having all sufficiency in all things may have abundance for every good work. (2 cor. 9:8).

We can attain the holiness that is required of us as children of light, if only we are ready for this period of transition, because that's where we miss it all. Waiting patiently for God is a big problem for the children of God. Recognizing the voice of Christ is another huge problem for us, because we have wandered so far away, we have been like sheep without a shepherd for too long, we have been masters of ourselves all these years of our lives without having anything but trouble, confusion, disappointment to show for it. We have tried to be masters of ourselves and failed. So it is time to hand our lives over to Christ Jesus the author and finisher of our faith.

When you buy a new product, there's usually a sheet of paper with instructions that the producer attached to the product. If you want the product to function well, you must have to read and follow the instructions carefully or else you may even damage what you bought with your money. But when you read and understand the instructions, all you need do is sit back, and enjoy it.

That is how God the producer of life, maker of heaven and earth has left us with sheets of instructions on life which is called the bible. He did this because he knows we don't know anything about life. He wants us to read it and follow the instructions we find in it so that we can sit back, and enjoy our lives. That is why God commanded Joshua to always meditate and speak the law of God. Let us have a look at the book of Joshua 1:8:—

This book of the law shall not depart out of thy mouth,

But thou shalt meditate therein day and night,
That thou mayest observe to do according to all that
Is written therein:for then thou shalt make thy ways
    prosperous,
And then thou shall have good success.

God did not keep anything secret because He wants us to be victorious and prosperous in every area of our lives. But the problem is that too many people thinks we cannot fellowship with him like ancient Israel did, but am here to tell you that God is willing to take us by the hand and bring us into His place of rest. He is only looking for empty vessels which He can work with.

I challenge you today to wake up from your sleep, pick up the manual of life, develop the habit of reading it every single day and you'll discover how sweet and simple God has made life.

Don't think it's too late to approach the throne of mercy because the book of Hebrews 4:1 says:—

> Let us beware, then:since the promise never lapses, none
> > of you must
> Think that he has come too late for the promise of
> > entering his place of rest.

That is why I love God; it's never too late. As long as you still have the breath of life in you and are ready to humble yourself in spirit and truth; you can meet with our Lord Jesus Christ.

Whatever you do today, always remember that God is waiting for you with open arms to return to the family of kings and priests that was purchased by the blood of Jesus Christ.

# Chapter 3

## True Repentance

"But now—declares Yahweh—
Come back to me with all your heart,
Fasting, weeping, mourning.
Tear your hearts and not your clothes.
And come back to Yahweh your God,
For he is gracious and compassionate,
Slow to anger, rich in faithful love,
And he relents about inflecting disaster.

That is the book of Joel 2:12-13:—

True repentance is of the heart. True repentance means having a change of heart. True repentance is like weighing your action on a two side scale and realizing that the ugly side of your life is heavier than the good side of your life. There and then the eyes of your heart open up and you realize how filthy and unworthy your actions had been, and you decide by the power of the Holy Spirit to make a change. Then a new birth takes place, the Holy Spirit comes into you instantly and you become a new born of the spirit of God.

True repentance is not about church attendance. It's not about how many times you can frequent the church, going to the church empty and coming out of the church emptier. True repentance is about forsaking your old sinful ways, realizing the love of God for you and reciprocating this love by being committed to the word of God; entrusting your life into the hands of God Almighty.

Our Lord Jesus made it clear in the book of Matthew 5:20

> For I say unto you, that except your righteousness exceeds that of
> The scribes and Pharisees, you shall in no case enter into the kingdom
> Of heaven.

When true repentance takes place you must hunger and thirst for righteousness, and only then shall you be filled (matt. 5:6). The light of God's word will shine on you as you determine to live in the presence of God.

The book of Genesis chapter 4 verse 3 to 7 says:—

> Now Abel became a shepherd and kept flocks, while Cain tilled
> The soil. Time passed and Cain brought some of the produce of the
> Soil as an offering for Yahweh, while Abel for his part brought the
> Firstborn of his flock and some of their fat as well. Yahweh looked

With favor on Abel and his offering. But he did not look with favor on Cain and his offering, and Cain was angry and downcast. Yahweh asked Cain 'why are you angry and downcast?' if you are doing right, surely you ought to hold your head high! But if you are not doing right, sin is crouching at the door, hungry to get you, you can still master him.

I would like you to reflect on verse 7 which says "but if you are not doing right, sin is crouching at your door, hungry to get you, you can still master him".

Think about this for a moment. God is telling us that sin is hungry to get us, to over shadow us, to dominate our lives, but because we are made in the image and likeness of God the father, because we have the breath of life in us, which is God's mighty presence in us, we can be masters over sin. We have the power within us to say yes or no to sin.

One of the things i love about God is the fact that he gives us the free will to decide what we want for our lives. He never impose anything on anyone; he never comes in till he is invited, even though he has the power to. When we choose to walk with him according to his word, everything he has made stands with and for us, the host of heaven backs us up, but when we choose to live in sin, he has no option but to stand aside and watch the enemy destroy us. His heart bleeds for our sake because he cannot save us, for we have built a wall of sin around us, which puts him off.

Genesis 17:1-3 reads:—when Abram was nighty-nine years old, Yahweh appeared to him and said, 'am the Almighty God; walk before me, and be thou perfect and i shall grant a covenant between myself and you, and make you very numerous. And Abram bowed to the ground.

One lovely thing about God is that He does not play hide and seek game, that's why he has given us simple instructions which we cannot follow by power or by might but by his spirit which humbles us.

God wants to see us make up our minds to walk in obedience according to his word. He wants to see us carry out his instructions. Sometimes, we obey his instructions, not because we can simply obey them but because we've learned to walk in obedience to his word.

We should always remember that our hearts are wide open before the living God. He sees our struggles, he sees our pains and how fears do torment us each time we are not spiritually equipped with the word of God.

For us to walk in perfection, we must put on the whole amour of God as apostle Paul advised us in the book of Ephesians 6:10-17.

If we want to participate as a chosen race, a holy nation, people of God's own pasture, we must reach perfection by staying away from sin.

God wants us to be perfect so that his plans for us will come into force, so that he can lavish his gifts on us and also fight our battles.

Our lord Jesus Christ himself said in the book of Luke chapter 6 verse 40;

> The disciple is not above his master!
> But everyone that is perfect shall be as his master.

Wao! What an eye opener! Christ Jesus gave us the secret of being like him.

As long as you keep feeding a child, that child must grow. So, as long as you keep feeding your mind and heart, the inner person with the word of God, the light of God's word shines in you. This makes it possible for you to resist the devil each time he comes around with temptations, and each time by the grace of God you resist the devil's temptations, he flees and you grow from glory to glory. If you go on with the word of God despite all odds, then God uplifts you to perfection.

We decide what we want to be in life, either to be hot for the lord or to be cold, or worse still to be lukewarm, but which ever be our decision we should always remember that without holiness no eye will see God. As long as we are still alive we have a blank check in our hands. We are to decide, either to spend them wisely or to spend them foolishly.

As for me, I have decided to live as God wants me to live. I have decided to reach perfection no matter what it takes; I will wait on the Lord.

I've discovered that waiting on the Lord patiently makes the devil so mad. I mean real mad. He knows he cannot beat you When you are patient. Have you noticed that when you are tolerant; because patience gives birth to tolerance, what you tolerate once, dares to repeat itself over and over again, and what you wait for patiently takes very long to come, but you feel the weight of all this when you do wait in the flesh and fight your battles yourself. But if you decide to wait patiently for God's own timing, you're to come out of whatsoever it is victoriously. So, patience is a powerful tool which leads us to perfection as recorded in the book of James 1:4:—

> But let patience have her perfect work,
> That you may be perfect and entire,
> Wanting nothing.

So, no matter what it takes, no matter what is happening to you and around you; know that they are all harassments and aggressions from the devil. But you can stop him as you wait patiently for the Lord in prayer, because it is not the will of God for you to live under pressure from the enemy. So, as long as it's not the will of God, you can drag the devil to the court of Heaven through prayer and you'll come out more than conquerors.

So put on the whole armor of God. Become spiritually aggressive and violent but at the same time humble in spirit, then you will see how God will destroy everything that has risen up against you and bring you out victoriously.

# Chapter 4

# Understanding the Power in the Word of God

I would like to begin this chapter with the book of genesis chapter 3:1-5

Now, the snake was the most subtle of all the wild animals that God made. It asked the woman, "did God really say you were not to eat from any of the tree in the garden?" The woman answered the snake, "we may eat the fruit of the trees in the garden, but of the fruit of the tree in the middle of the garden God said, "you must not eat it, nor touch it, under pain of death." Then the snake said to the woman, no! You will not die!, God knows in fact that the day you eat it your eyes will be opened and you will be like gods, knowing good from evil.

Our problem with God Almighty is understanding. He clearly says in the book of Hosea 4:6 "My people are destroyed for lack of knowledge". We do not have deep knowledge of the word of God, this makes us not to understand his word.

Our lack of knowledge makes us not to understand him when He speaks to us, just like Adam and Eve.

When God told Adam that any day he eat the fruit from the tree in the middle of the garden he would die, he (Adam) did not understand that God was talking about spiritual death. The devil himself also did not understand that God was not talking about physical death, even though it is a part of it

God was talking about man living his life without God's friendship and intimacy.

If you do not live according to the word of God, you lack these God given rights mentioned above; you're dead spiritually even though you are still physically alive.

I was listening to a preacher one day and she made mention of the book of Matthew 10:7-8 which says:—and as ye go preach, saying the kingdom of God is at hand. Heal the sick, cleanse the lepers, and raise the dead, cast out devils. Freely ye have received freely give.

At the mention of these words, i was caught up in my thoughts, thinking and at the same time asking myself how this verse of the scripture could come to pass in every believer's life. I was asking myself; "how can every child of God raise the dead to life"? Then i heard the holy spirit telling me these words:—why do you people think that it's only lifeless bodies that are dead? And he continued by saying "do you know that if you are able to make a single person have a change of heart with the word of God, you have raised that person back to life!

I was so shocked about the lesson i received from the Holy Spirit and I instantly understood how God loves us and is so willing and ready to teach us the things of the spirit, anytime, anywhere.

Likewise one other day, i was meditating on the word of God which says "God is the same yesterday, today and forever ", while i was wondering in my thoughts i asked myself "how is it possible that God is the same yesterday today and forever?, and suddenly the answer came which says, "Because yesterday, today and forever does not exist in the spiritual realm, the only thing that exist in the spiritual realm is now"!

My spirit was awakened and instantly I understood why we perish for lack of knowledge and understanding of the word of God. We perish because we are empty and God has nothing in us to work with, he has nothing to hold onto in order to increase our knowledge.

The book of Hebrews 4:12 says:—The word of God is alive and active, and is quicker and sharper than any two edged sword.

So when we lack the word of God, we lack the life and activeness that comes along with it. Everything that is seen and unseen were made by these same word, the same word became alive and dwelt amongst us as recorded in the book of john 1:14.

When we lack the word of God in us that means we lack Christ Jesus in the inside of us and we become dried and anything dried does not bring forth fresh fruits. That's why he said in the book of john 14:6:—I am the way, the truth, and the life; no man cometh to the father, but by me.

So, when we lack the word of God, we lack Christ Jesus which is life = being dead, even though we are still breathing and walking about. When we know the word of God and live by it, springs of living water will begin to flow from the inside of us as Christ said in the book of john 7:38:—He that believeth on me, as the scripture hath said, out of his belly shall flow rivers of living water. So it's time we give every other thing up for the word of God. It's time to say to God, "father into your hands i commit my body, soul and spirit", as Jesus Christ said on the cross. Only then will God take over our affairs and walk with us in a pillar of fire by night and a pillar of cloud by day.

Abraham is a perfect example when you talk about understanding the word of God. I would like you to think of what would have become of Abraham if he was unable to hear God's voice when he spoke to him or if he was unable to understand that God was talking to him.

Think of what would have become of Abraham! He might not have discovered the friendship of God, he might not have known God as Jehovah Jireh, he might not have been the vessel with which God established an everlasting covenant which is valid forever and is available for you and i to tap into anytime we are willing and obedient.

When God created the heaven and the earth, the earth was without form and void, and darkness was upon the face of the deep. And the spirit of God moved upon the face of the waters. And God said, let there be light:and there was light. (Genesis 1:1-3).

Light did not just appear, but because God spoke in confidence of himself, having full knowledge of whom he is. He called forth light and it appeared. He had no doubt if what he said would be possible or not because he taught of it before declaring it, so also should we always come to him with joy and gladness knowing that if we ask anything in the name of his dear son Jesus Christ without doubt in our hearts that we shall receive that which we ask of.

If you have knowledge of anything at all, you'll have confidence in yourself when you deal with that particular thing or situation.

When you have knowledge of the word of God, when you have yourself enwrapped with the word of God, you'll be in Christ Jesus and him in you, then you will speak with assurance, power and authority.

Remember that knowledge is the information you contain in you. So, when you have the knowledge of the word of God, you contain the word of the living God in you. The book of john 1:1-5, 1 4 says "In the beginning was the word, and the word was with God, and the word was God. The same was in the beginning with God. All things were made by him, and without him was nothing made that was made. In him was life, and the life was the light of men. And the light shineth in darkness and the darkness comprehended it not.

And the word was made flesh, and dwelt among us, (and we beheld his glory, the glory as the only begotten of the father,) full of grace and truth.

This passage is telling us that Jesus Christ is the word of God. God Almighty made his word to become flesh. So, like i was saying before, and in connection with the scripture we've just read, we find out that when you have the knowledge of the word of God, it means that you contain the word of God on the inside of you, which means you contain Christ Jesus in the inside of you! Jesus Christ dwells in you!!

And you must know that you are a well and out of you shall flow rivers of living water (John 7:38). Remember that the word of God is alive and active, quicker and sharper than any two-edged sword, it can seek out the place where soul is divided from the spirit or joints from marrow, it can pass judgment on secret emotions and thoughts. (Hebrews 4:12-13).

When you have the word of God in you, you are a container of something that values more than diamond, something that worth more than gold. The only thing you have to do is to build a wall around your heart in order not to allow doubt come in. That is why it is written in the book of proverbs 4:23 that we should guide our hearts with all diligence, cause out of it flows the issues of life. So, all you really need to do is guide your heart with the word of God, then declare the word of God with faith over every moment of your life, over every situation you come across. You have to speak the word of God out into thin air. You must bear in mind that as you have ears, eyes and other senses, that's how situation has these senses as well.

When you speak the word of God, you are sending Jesus Christ forth into your situation. You must have to continue to speak the word of God over any situation you do not agree with as long as it takes. I tell you, as long as God is God, that situation must give way, not because it wants to, but because the word of God (Christ Jesus) has come against it.

Your lack of knowledge of the word of God means your lack of life (meaning being dead), and could also be called "lack of identity "because when Jesus is not in you (the word), there's no way you can have the experience of being a chosen generation, a royal priesthood, a holy nation, a peculiar people; that you should show forth the praises of him who hath called you out of darkness into his marvelous light. (1 peter 2:9).

Your lack of the knowledge of the word of God keeps you from receiving from God. Until you change your position from lack of knowledge to full of knowledge of the word of God, you'll always be empty and live in the cycle of lack of identity.

Knowledge is very important in our walk with the Lord. If we don't have the knowledge of our inheritance in Christ, we cannot make any impact on those around us and the world as a whole.

The same spirit God gave to Adam from the very beginning, his image and likeness that is the same spirit we have in us.

Adam knew he had authority to name the animals as he wished (Genesis 2:19). Before the fall of man, Adam knew God, he knew how to fellowship with God. He knew his inheritance.

One thing about God is that he's so generous to the extent of leaving us signed open checks. He said, "just fill in anything you need and it will be yours", but too many Christians are ignorant of this fact because they don't find it necessary to study the word of God, too many Christians are robbed of their inheritance in the kingdom of God because of their ignorance of the word of God.

The steps of the righteous are ordered by the Lord:and he delighted in his ways. (Psalm 37:23). The Lord will order your steps only through the knowledge of his word which is stored in you. If you are ignorant of the word of God, i want you to know that you've missed the whole concept of life.

# Chapter 5

# Believing and the word of God

Judges. 6:12-13 and the angel of the lord appeared unto him, and said unto him, the Lord is with thee, thou mighty man of valor. and Gideon said unto him, oh my lord, if the Lord be with us, why then is all this befallen us? And where be all his miracles which our fathers told us of saying, did not the Lord bring us up from Egypt? But now the Lord hath forsaken us, and delivered us into the hands of the Midianites.

You might be found in the same situation which Gideon found himself when the angel of the lord visited him and are wondering in your thoughts; do God still do miracles? Or you might be one of those that really believe that the miracles we do read of in the bible can no longer take place in our lives today.

But whatever you're going through today does not make you anything lesser than whom God has already made you, but rather God allows some situations into your life as stepping stones to your place of rest. A ladder to the higher place he is taking you to.

I really want you to know that God is not a respecter of persons but a respecter of his word. Once you live and ask according to his word, he releases the answer to your prayers.

God wants us to see ourselves the way he sees us:—wonderfully and fearfully made in the image and likeness of God. Joint heirs with Christ Jesus.

God wants us to take every obstacle that has been hindering his fatherly love for his, out of the way. He wants us to take away every bitterness, every form of unforgiveness, every pride, jealousy, prayerlessness and the rest of the things that are not of the Lord, because these are not the fruit of the spirit. As you cut down these evil trees which the enemy of our souls has planted in your heart as God commanded Gideon.

> And it came to pass the same night, that the lord said
>     unto him,
> Take thy father's young bullock, even the second bullock
>     of seven years old,
> And throw down the altar of ball that thy father hath,
> And cut down the grove that is by it. (Judges 6:25).

When you cut these evil trees which stands in between you and God, then you'll have to replace them with the word of God which is Jesus Christ, you must hate and run away from sin because that is the only thing that can separate you from the love of God. Only then can you bear the fruit of the spirit which is love, joy, peace, patience, kindness, goodness, trustfulness, gentleness and self-control; no law can touch such thing as these. All who belong to Christ Jesus have crucified self with all its passions and it's desires. (Galatians 5:22-24).

# The Blood of Jesus

One day as i was meditating on the word of God, the Holy Spirit revealed an uncommon secret to me. He said; "Do you know that anytime you go into battle (you decide to live your moments of discomfort praising God) with full consciousness of who you are in Christ Jesus, whatever is surrounding the need you're praying for gives way, because the devil and his demons knows who you are? Then i said Lord, what are you telling me? He said "warfare".

That is how it is with the blood of Jesus. If only you know the power in the blood of Jesus that has brought you into the kingdom of God and made you the righteousness of God in Christ Jesus according to the book of 2 Corinthians 5:21, you will be happy in the Lord Jesus all through your life time, regardless of the circumstances surrounding you.

The book of Matthew 27:50-53 states:—

Jesus, when he had cried again with a loud voice, yielded up the ghost. And, behold, the veil of the temple was rent in twain from the top to the bottom:and the earth did quake, and the rock rent:and the graves were opened; and many bodies of the saints which slept arose. And came out of the graves after his resurrection and went into the holy city, and appeared unto many.

Jesus cried the first time at about the ninth hour saying "God, my God, why hast thou forsaken me". in the book of Matthew 27:46, nothing happened because the blood had not yet been shed, but immediately he died, the power in his blood came into force. Chapter 51 states that the veil in the temple tore into two.

When the veil tore into two, we gained access into the throne room of God. This veil was in-between the inner court and the most holy place, where the priests offer sacrifices to God our father for the sins of the Israelites, and where no other person can go into except the priests, but the very second Christ paid for our sins with his blood, that veil was divided into two parts, giving us a direct view of the most holy place of God (Hebrews 10:19).

Christ Jesus by his death became our spiritual veil (Hebrews 10:20), that is why the physical veil was torn by the power of God, because the spiritual veil has come into force. Christ is the spiritual veil because he is the only mediator between God and Man.

The earth quaked and the rock rented because the transformation had taken place. Everything God had in plan for us got connected at that very second that the blood of Jesus was shed. God reconciled us to himself and we became partakers of his divine nature (2 peter 1:4).

The shed blood of Jesus reconciled us with God once and for all, unlike the blood of goats and calves which was shed once every year by the high priest (Hebrew 9:7), but Christ became our high priest by shedding his blood once and for all, and for this cause he is the mediator of the new testament as written in the book of Hebrews 9:15. Let us read:—for this reason Christ is the mediator of a new covenant, that those who are called may receive the promised eternal inheritance—now that he has died as a ransom to set free from the sins committed under the first covenant.

So, we should stop acting like slaves begging from the master and start acting like sons asking from their father. God the father is calling us through every means he can reach us because he wants us to spend eternity with him in his kingdom where everything is the way he has made them, with no intruder to turn things upside down.

God the father is much more than we think of him, that is why he can do exceedingly, abundantly and above all we can think or ask of him (Ephesians 3:20).

God wants us to approach him with all boldness knowing he can never go back to his words. We must always remember that God is not a man that he should lie, neither a son of man that he should repent.

We must also know that the blood of Jesus is all that is needed to restore us to son ship, and since the blood is available to those that are willing, i refuse to act like an orphan because am a child of the most high God, wonderfully and fearfully made in his likeness and image and having thousands of angels of God at my disposal to bring the word of God to pass in every area of my life.

What about you? How do you see yourself? A helpless or worthless person? Then you are qualified for the blessings of God our father, because our lord Jesus did not come for the needless but for the needy. So this is the appointed time for you to meet with the lord Jesus, embrace him through his words and never let him go then he will bless you, amen.

# Chapter 6

# Accepting Responsibility

God expects us to take responsibility for our actions. He wants us to be spiritually matured because that's what it takes to be responsible.

God the father showed us the example of maturity and responsibility by not laying any blame on Adam for not obeying his instructions, but he took the necessary time that he needed to find the solution to the disaster, he took time to find the only needed solution that will last for all eternity. That is our lord Jesus Christ, who died once and for all, a perfect sacrifice.

When you pass through moments of discomfort, which most of the times is attracted by sin, all you need do is to accept you have sinned, be sorry for what you have done and be ready to bear the pains that will be attracted by that sin because they will surely come. But you should also bear in mind as you accept your sins, that God is merciful, loving and kind. Whatever He allows you to pass through is for your own good and because He loves you. You can read the book of 1 chronicles 21:1, 7-8, 12-13, 15 and 17. This will help you understand clearly how you can handle situations such as this.

When all hope is gone; you've tried all you possibly can but you still find a thick wall of impossibility between you and the solution to your problem, all you need do is to remember that God is there waiting for you to realize your mistakes, and ask for the forgiveness of your sins and wait on the lord to deliver you. We should always be conscious of the devil and his tricks. We should also know that sin is the only thing that opens the door for the devil to come into our lives.

Knowing our nature, God tries in different ways to get our attention, so we can come back to him, because that's the only thing that can keep us safe.

Let us take a look at the book of genesis 16:3-9:—

And Sarai Abram's wife took Hagar her maid the Egyptian, after Abram had dwelt ten years in the land of Canaan, and gave her to her husband Abram to be his wife.

And he went in unto Hagar, and she conceived, and when she saw that she had conceived, her mistress was despised in her eyes. and Sarai said unto Abram, my wrong be upon thee, i have given my maid into thy bosom; and when she saw that she had conceived, i was despised in her eyes:the lord judge between me and thee. but Abram said unto Sarai, behold, thy maid is in thy hand; do to her as it pleaseth thee. And when Sarai dealt hardly with her, she fled from her face. and the angel of the lord found her by a fountain of water in the wilderness, by the fountain in the way to shur. and he said, Hagar, Sarai's maid, whence camest thou?

And whither wilt thou go? And she said, i flee from my the face of my mistress Sarai. and the angel of the Lord said unto her, return to thy mistress, and submit thyself under her hands. as the angel of the Lord said to Hagar," return to thy mistress, and submit thyself under her hands". That's how God wants us to go back to the root of our problems by accepting responsibility, by coming to full consciousness that sin has opened the door for the enemy of our soul to attack us. God the father wants us to know that he is always waiting to hear our cry for help if we call on him sincerely, if we call on him without laying blame on anyone at all. He wants us to realize that the enemy of our soul is the devil who comes to steal, kill and destroy us but Jesus come that we might have life and have it more abundantly.

Sometimes also, God puts us to the test not to condemn or forsake us but to reveal our weaknesses to us. So in your walk with Lord, you should always keep your spiritual senses sharp and alive so you can discern times and seasons. Always remember that these times shall come when God might decide to take you through the fire. I said take you through the fire because whatever you go through, he is always there with you. I know this because he has promised never to leave you nor forsake you. So when discomfort comes around all you need do is to keep your spiritual ears wide open so you can hear the holy spirit clearly and don't forget that God is always by your side watching to see if you will obey his word or not, just like he did with Abraham in the book of genesis 22:1-8:—and it came to pass after these things, that God did tempt Abraham, and said unto him, Abraham:and he said, behold, here i am. and he said, take now thy son, thy only son. Isaac, whom thou lovest, and get thee into the land of Moriah; and offer him there for a burnt offering upon one of the mountains which i will tell thee of. and Abraham rose up early in the morning and saddled his ass and took two of his young men with him, and Isaac his son, and clave the wood for the burnt offering, and rose up, and went unto the place of which God had told him. then on the third day Abraham lifted up his eyes, and saw the place after off. and Abraham said unto his men, abide ye here with the ass; i and the lad will go yonder and worship, and come again to you. and Abraham took the wood of the burnt offering, and laid it upon Isaac his son; and he took the fire in his hand, and a knife; and they went both of them together. and Isaac spake unto Abraham his father, and said, my father:and he said, here am i my son. And he said, behold the fire and the wood:but where is the lamb for a burnt offering? and Abraham said, my son, God will provide himself a lamb for a burnt offering:so they went both of them together.

God's original intension when he made this request to Abraham was to really know if Abraham loved him. And Abraham demonstrated his love for God and early the next morning to do what was required of him by the Lord. If you love the Lord, you must live according to his words. If Abraham had not obeyed God completely, God would not have sworn by himself to bless Abraham with the blessing that has been extended to you and i today and forever. So each time we pass through trials and temptations, we should always remember that sorrow may endure all through the night but joy cometh in the morning (Psalm 30:5). We must always remember that God has a better plan for us which we know nothing of, for us to come out of our troubles victoriously, we must always think of the power and greatness of the most high God in every moment of our lives. We must speak positive words which flows from our hearts, because as a man thinks in his heart, so is he. We must hold unto our faith in God knowing that with God all things are possible. Above all, we, in times of trouble must bring to God sacrifices of praise and thanksgiving, and also we must be convinced that He is the God that can do exceedingly abundantly above all we can think and ask of him. Abraham's word of confidence in God to Isaac his son in genesis 22 verse 8 touched the heart of God. Abraham knew that even if he sacrificed Isaac as a burnt offering, God had a better plan for him. That is why he spoke confidently about God, and in return God answered him instantly. He walked by faith and not by sight.

Imagine yourself in a situation, a very bad one, and the only thing that can see you through is God's intervention. All what you need do is to believe the word of God and hold on to your faith, be calm in the spirit so as to be physically calm, and develop your spiritual muscles. Always remember that you must pass through to get a breakthrough. Praying and singing songs of praise to God are very powerful weapons to destroy worries in every uncomfortable moment. As you sing and pray you'll witness God's divine intervention.

I urge you to read the rest of genesis chapter 22, so that you can understand the blessings that followed Abraham's obedience to God.

The choice is yours; to turn each moment of trial to a stumbling block or a stepping stone.

I would like us to take note of acts of irresponsibility that took place between Esau and Jacob in the book of genesis 25:29-34

Once when Jacob was cooking a stew, and Esau came from the field, and he was faint. and Esau said to Jacob, feed me, i pray thee, with that same portage, for i am faint:therefor was his name called Edom. and Jacob said, sell me this day thy birth—right. and Esau said, behold, i am at the point to die:and what profit shall this birthright do to me. and Jacob said, swear to me this day; and he sware unto him:and sold his birthright unto Jacob. then Jacob gave Esau bread and pottage of lentils:and he did eat and drink and rose up; and went his way:thus Esau despised his birthright.

I would like you to go through these verses once more and take a moment to reflect over why Esau had to sell his birthright, his God given position within a twinkle of an eye, without any sense of responsibility. Unfortunately that's how many Christians whom God the father has bought over to himself with the precious blood of Jesus has lost their heritage through acts of irresponsibility. That is how many Christians, people of God's own pasture, people called by the name of the Lord has consciously or unconsciously handed over to Satan, the enemy of our souls; their God given birthright in Christ through unbelief, lack of patience, knowledge and understanding, just because they do not really know their God given position.

If you want to see God at work in your affairs, you must have to do what Esau never thought of doing; staying without food than selling your heritage in Christ Jesus, then you will see Jehovah Jireh, the provider of all things providing for you according to his riches in glory by Christ Jesus.

When in your times of discomfort you praise God, you are being faithful like job. If you are steadfast in faith no matter what comes your way, God will bring you through to the end and crown you with joy and satisfaction. He will restore whatsoever that has Been stolen from you just like he did for job. So quit crying, complaining and murmuring today and start praising the Lord for counting you worthy to partake in his divine plan.

If you've already known the Lord but there is lack, health problems or anything you might be going through, God wants you to keep these problems beside and not before you, so they would not become stumbling blocks on your way to where God is taking you to.

All you need do is to feed your spirit with the word of God, remind God in prayers of his promises and never allow doubt to get anywhere close to your heart. Never accept any solution that is not from the lord because they are temporal.

When you encounter problems, life's challenges, God wants you to be still so he can show you his salvation. Always remember that he knows all what is happening in your life.

If you sturdy the bible constantly you'll come across thousands of promises which God has made to us concerning every single need. Remember his word which says "many trouble befall the righteous but the Lord God delivers him from them all not one of his bones are broken "(Psalm 34:19). He knows about whatever the devil is doing to you, so you should pray without ceasing as you wait patiently and happily for the Lord in prayer.

I said happily because you decide either to be happy all the times, despite what is happening around you or to be sad all the time. In case you've chosen to be sad, or complain and murmur as you wait, i would like you to know that the battle you are into may never be over because sadness, complaining, murmuring are like fuel to your battles. They are the engines that moves your battles against you.

I will also like to take a few lines to talk about fear. The spirit of fear is so deadly that it will keep you imprisoned without your knowledge. It is the deadliest weapon the devil has, and he attacks the children of the living God with it. When the spirit of fear comes in, you act and react without the spirit of discernment. So many wrong decisions has been taken by Christians under the pressure of fear, and 90% of the decisions taken in fears turns out to be wrong.

As for me, no condition can steal my joy because I have decided that nothing can separate me from the love of God. Living joyfully and happily is a choice and what strengthens me each day is the book of Romans 8:35-39:—

> Who shall separate us from the love of Christ? Shall tribulation, or
> Distress, or persecution, or famine, or nakedness, or peril, or sword?
> As it written, for thy sake we are killed all the day long; we are accounted
> As sheep for the slaughter.
> No, in all these things we are more than conquerors through him that loved us.
> For I am persuaded, that neither death, nor life, nor angels, nor principalities,
> Nor powers, nor things present, nor things to come,
> Nor height, nor depth, nor any other creature, shall be able to separate us from
> The love of God, which is in Christ Jesus our Lord.
> If you live your life with this mindset; you will end each day of your life joyfully and victoriously.

# Chapter 7

# The Spirit of Discernment

## What is discernment?

To discern means to see and identify by nothing, a difference or differences; to note the distinctive character of; to distinguish.

Or

To see by the eye or by the understanding, to perceive and recognize; as to discern a difference.

Or

To make distinction between good and evil, truth and falsehood.

Let's take a look at the book of 1 kings 3:7-14:—

And now, Lord my God, thou hast made thy servant king instead of David my father:and i am but a little child:i know not how to go out or come in and thy servant is in the mist of thy people which thou has chosen, a great people, that cannot be numbered nor counted for multitude. give therefore an understanding heart to judge thy people, that i may discern between good and bad:for who is able to judge this thy so great a people? and the speech pleased the Lord, that Solomon had asked this thing. and God said unto him, because thou hast ask this thing, and hast not asked for thyself long life; neither has asked riches for thyself, nor hast thou asked for the life of thy enemies; but has asked for thyself understanding and discern judgment. behold, i have done according to thy words:lo, i have given thee a wise and understanding heart; so that there was none like thee before thee, neither after thee shall any arise like unto thee. and i have also given thee that which thou hast not asked, both riches and honor; so that there shall not be any among the kings like unto thee all thy days. and if thou wilt walk in my ways, to keep my statues and my commandments, as thy father David did walk, then i will lengthen thy days.

I would like you to read this chapter again and carefully and spend time to meditate on them because in them are hidden some powerful secrets to the heart of God.

If you lack the spirit of discernment, it means you are spiritually blunt because this very word "discern "has a real lot to do in our Christian lives.

You need the spirit of discernment to make distinction between good and evil. You need the spirit of discernment to understand times and seasons you are living in. You need the spirit of discernment to know when to rise up in prayer and when to sing only praises to the Lord. You need the spirit of discernment to understand when you have prayed enough, when it's time to hand the battle over to the Lord, rest, and stand still to see the salvation of the Lord.

Most time we are the ones that turns our lives upside down because we don't understand when we should walk or run, when we should raise a war cry and get heaven's attention, or when we should only sing praises to God telling him we know his thoughts for us is for good and not for evil, and no matter what we are passing through, we know he will give us an expected end.

That is why the children of the most high God are not swimming in the ocean of miracles, because without discerning the times and season, it will be impossible for us to have a tangible fruit to show for our obedience to the word of God. Take for instance a farmer; he knows when to weed the grass and when to sow the seeds. Imagine if he should be sowing during harvest time! That's what majority of the Christians do. They cry when they should be laughing because of what the Lord God is about to do in their lives. They quit and cry when they should mount up with wings like Eagles. They walk like blind people into the pit which the devil has dug for them without realizing it, all because they cannot discern what is happening to them. They neither know where they are nor where they are going to. Without the spirit to discern, we are lost!

The problem with the children of the most high God is that we give up too soon in every battle all because we are not all ways able to discern the tricks of the devil. If we can learn to listen to the spirit, i tell you the devil can never beat us in any way. You must know that the devil hides behind your ignorance to attack you. He only takes the space you give him.

# Let Us Pray:

Heavenly father, I thank you for your word which is alive, and I also thank you for giving me this opportunity to draw closer to you once again.

Thank you for the power in the blood of Jesus which is available to me.

Thank you once again for loving me. I also ask you to give me the grace to love you too through our Lord Jesus Christ.

I ask you lord to help me to be not only a hearer of your word but also a doer of your life—giving word, so that I will bear the fruits of the spirit to your honor and glory, in Jesus name.

I ask you Lord to be my light and my salvation.

I present myself to you as a living sacrifice; may I be acceptable in your sight in Jesus name.

I also come to you as an empty vessel. Fill me with the peace and joy that comes from your name.

Thank you father for every single thing which you have done in my life and the new thing you are about to do. In Jesus name I pray, amen.